TABLE OF CONTENTS

CHAPTER 1

SENECA FALLS

On July 19, 1848, around 300 women and men met in a church. It was in Seneca Falls, New York. They spoke about women's **rights** and suffrage. This is the right to **vote**. At the time, only men could vote.

TURNING POINTS IN U.S. HISTORY

WOMEN'S SUFFRAGE MOVEMENT

by Veronica B. Wilkins

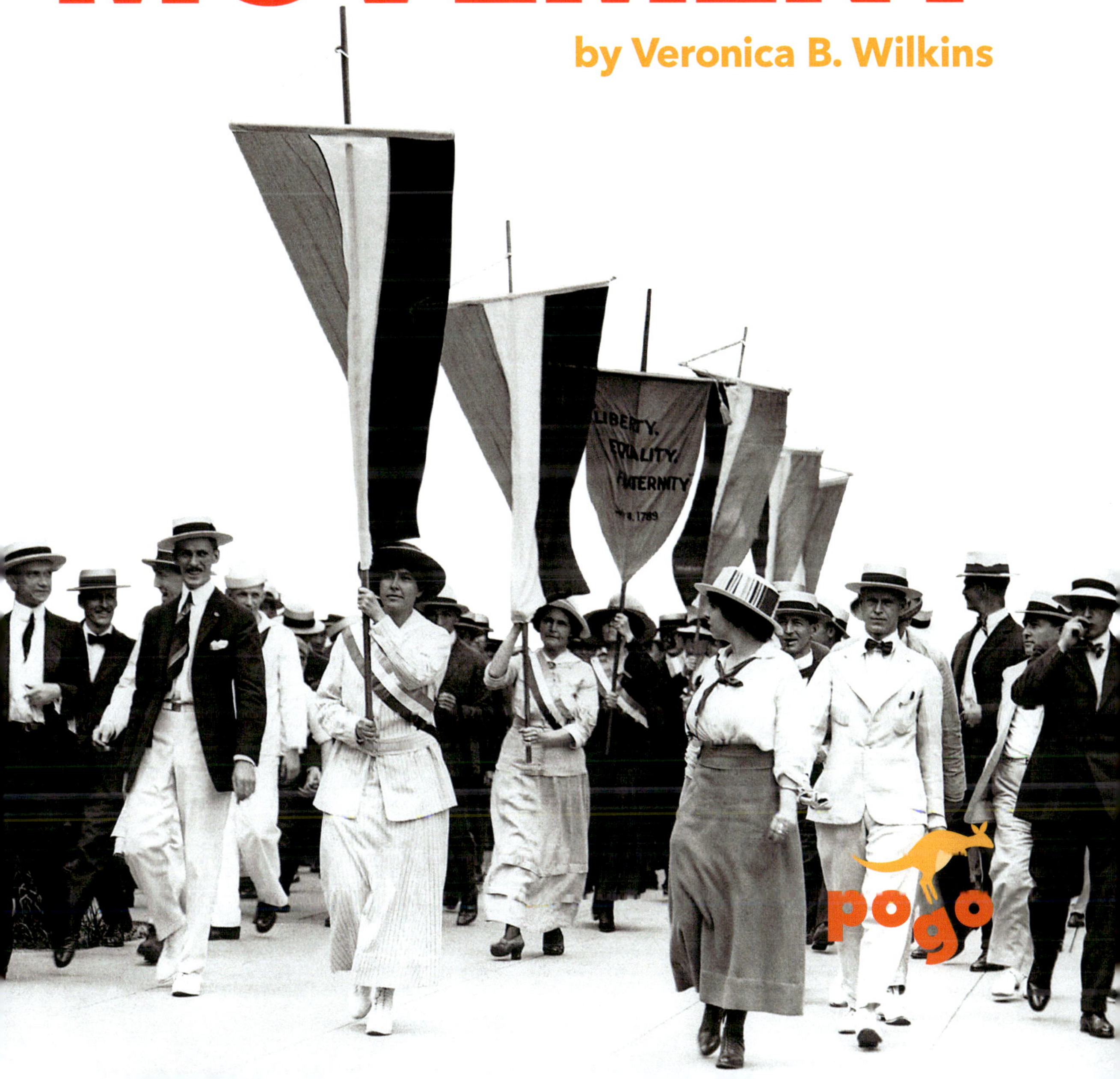

pogo

Ideas for Parents and Teachers

Pogo Books let children practice reading informational text while introducing them to nonfiction features such as headings, labels, sidebars, maps, and diagrams, as well as a table of contents, glossary, and index.

Carefully leveled text with a strong photo match offers early fluent readers the support they need to succeed.

Before Reading

- "Walk" through the book and point out the various nonfiction features. Ask the student what purpose each feature serves.
- Look at the glossary together. Read and discuss the words.

Read the Book

- Have the child read the book independently.
- Invite him or her to list questions that arise from reading.

After Reading

- Discuss the child's questions. Talk about how he or she might find answers to those questions.
- Prompt the child to think more. Ask: Women worked for a long time for the right to vote. What would you work to change?

Pogo Books are published by Jump!
5357 Penn Avenue South
Minneapolis, MN 55419
www.jumplibrary.com

Library of Congress Cataloging-in-Publication Data

Names: Wilkins, Veronica B., 1994- author.
Title: Women's suffrage movement / Veronica B. Wilkins.
Description: Pogo books.
Minneapolis, MN: Jump!, Inc, 2020.
Series: Turning points in U.S. history
Includes bibliographical references and index.
Audience: Ages 7-10.
Identifiers: LCCN 2019021571 (print)
LCCN 2019980746 (ebook)
ISBN 9781645271444 (hardcover)
ISBN 9781645271451 (paperback)
ISBN 9781645271468 (ebook)
Subjects: LCSH: Women–Suffrage
United States–History–Juvenile literature.
Suffragists–United States History–Juvenile literature.
Classification: LCC JK1898 .W55 2020 (print)
LCC JK1898 (ebook) | DDC 324.6/230973–dc23
LC record available at https://lccn.loc.gov/2019021571
LC ebook record available at https://lccn.loc.gov/2019980746

Editor: Susanne Bushman
Designer: Jenna Casura

Photo Credits: Everett Historical/Shutterstock, cover, 1, 12-13, 17, 18-19, 23; Ken Florey Suffrage Collection/Gado/Getty, 3; Epics/Getty, 4; Wavebreakmedia/iStock, 5 (background); Bettmann/Getty, 5 (foreground); F.L. Stuber/Library of Congress/Corbis/Getty, 6-7; Topical Press Agency/Getty, 8-9; Bain News Service/Library of Congress, 10, 14-15; George Grantham Bain Collection/Library of Congress, 11; Mansell/The LIFE Picture Collection/Getty, 16; Tom Williams/CQ Roll Call/Getty, 20-21.

Printed in the United States of America at Corporate Graphics in North Mankato, Minnesota.

Elizabeth Cady Stanton and Lucretia Mott led the meeting. They wanted a say in the country's laws. But to have that, they needed to vote. So they fought for suffrage. We call these women suffragettes.

Many women during this time stayed home. Their job was to care for children. Their husbands worked.

Some women, like Stanton and Mott, were active in **politics**. They fought against **slavery**. They learned to speak to crowds. They learned to write well. U.S. slavery ended after the Civil War (1861–1865). Women began using what they learned to fight for suffrage.

women's club
WOMENS CHRISTIAN TEMPERANCE UNION

Many women's clubs formed in the late 1800s. These groups educated women. Some worked to change laws. A ban on alcohol was one. As these groups grew, more women joined suffrage groups, too.

CHAPTER 2

WORKING FOR CHANGE

Women **protested**. They marched on foot through the streets. Some rode horses. They held signs. Some decorated cars. They even wore costumes.

The first march was in 1910. People watched marches. Newspapers wrote about them. The marches grew. In 1913, around 8,000 women marched in Washington, D.C. In 1915, 40,000 women marched in New York City.

Washington, D.C. march

Suffragettes **campaigned**. How? They wrote newspapers. They gave out fliers. They spoke out, too. They talked to politicians. They gave speeches. They gave reasons for women's suffrage.

WHAT DO YOU THINK?

Susan B. Anthony was a famous suffragette. She talked a man into letting her vote. She was **arrested**. Would you have done this? Why or why not?

flier

Suffragettes campaigned in each state. Why? States could make their own laws. Their work paid off in Wyoming first. The **territory** gave women the right to vote in 1869. In 1916, the first woman was elected to **Congress**. Her name was Jeannette Rankin.

TAKE A LOOK!

Women first won suffrage in Wyoming. Many states followed. What year could women vote in your state?

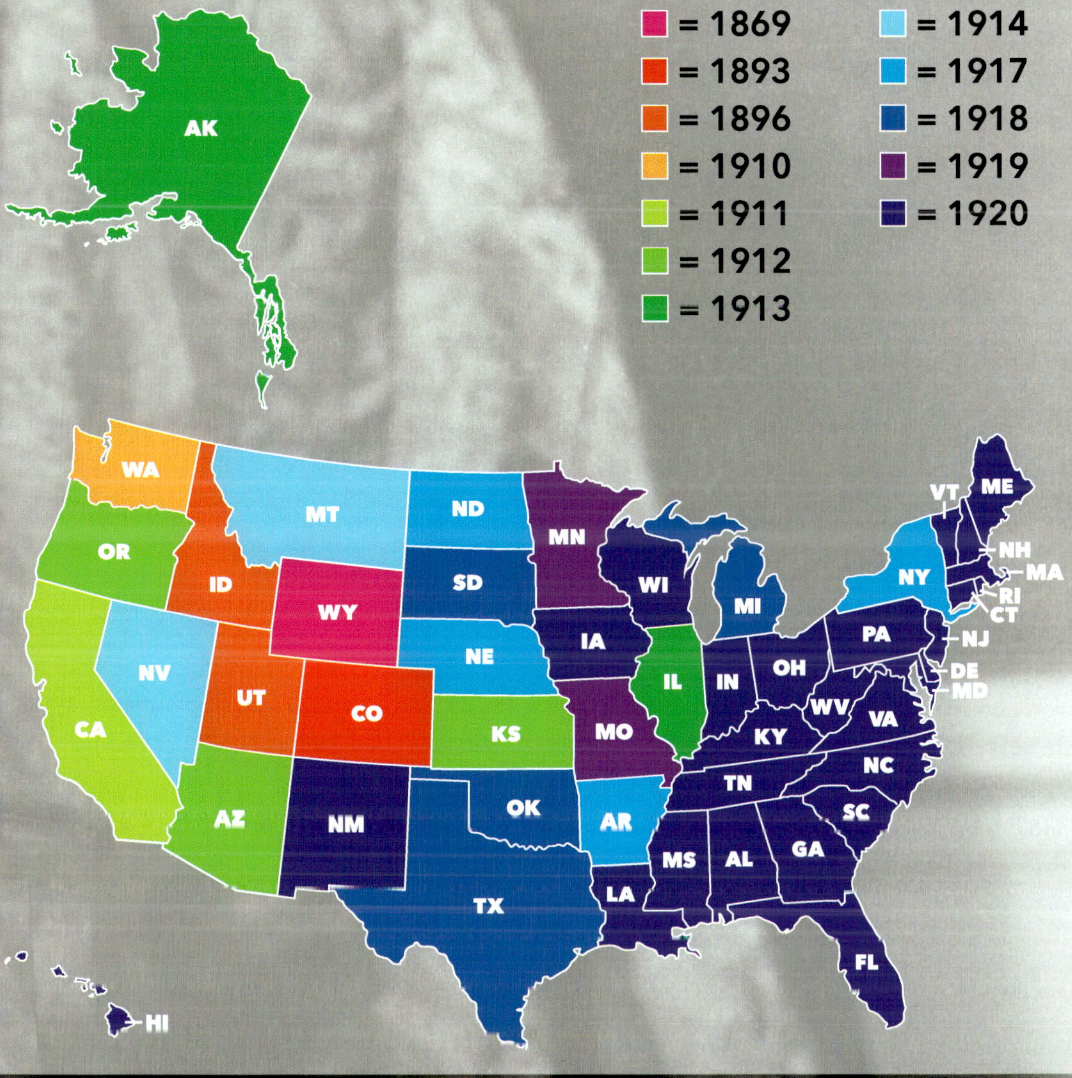

CHAPTER 3

SUFFRAGE IS WON

World War I (1914–1918) called many men to war. Women filled the jobs they left behind. This helped suffragettes. How? It showed that women cared for their country just as men did.

But there was still work to do. Protests continued. Suffragettes **picketed** the White House. Many were arrested.

passing of the Nineteenth Amendment

Finally, the president helped. Woodrow Wilson asked Congress to change the law. This was on September 30, 1918. It took nearly two years, but the law changed. The Nineteenth Amendment passed on August 18, 1920. It said women could vote!

DID YOU KNOW?

President Wilson was not the first man to help. Men were at Seneca Falls. Suffragettes' husbands helped. There was a Men's League for Women's Suffrage.

Women fought for suffrage for more than 70 years. Their work changed America forever.

Today, women have had the right to vote for about 100 years! Many women work in government, too. In 2018, a record was set. The most women ever were elected to Congress!

WHAT DO YOU THINK?

Women fought for a voice in politics. What if they hadn't done this? How would it feel if you did not have a voice?

female
Congress members

QUICK FACTS & TOOLS

TIMELINE

July 19, 1848
The Seneca Falls Convention takes place as the first women's rights convention.

December 6, 1865
The Thirteenth Amendment abolishes, or ends, slavery.

December 10, 1869
The Territory of Wyoming allows women to vote.

November 5, 1872
Susan B. Anthony illegally votes in New York.

May 21, 1910
The first women's suffrage march takes place in New York City.

October 23, 1915
Around 40,000 women march for suffrage in New York City.

November 7, 1916
Jeannette Rankin becomes the first woman elected to Congress.

September 30, 1918
President Woodrow Wilson speaks to Congress, stating his support for a women's suffrage amendment.

August 18, 1920
The Nineteenth Amendment grants women the right to vote.

August 18, 2020
Women have been able to vote in the United States for 100 years.

GLOSSARY

arrested: Stopped and held by the power of the law.

campaigned: Conducted a series of connected acts to bring about a certain result.

Congress: The lawmaking body of the United States, made up of the Senate and the House of Representatives.

picketed: Protested by walking or standing in front of something.

politics: The activity and discussions involved in governing a country, state, or city.

protested: Demonstrated against something.

rights: Things you are legally or morally entitled to do.

slavery: A system in which people are owned by other people and are forced to work without pay.

territory: An area of the United States that is not part of a state but has an organized, separate government.

vote: To cast a ballot, making a choice in an election.

INDEX

TO LEARN MORE

Finding more information is as easy as 1, 2, 3.

1. Go to www.factsurfer.com
2. Enter "women'ssuffragemovement" into the search box.
3. Choose your book to see a list of websites.

FACT SURFER